Living in the truth

The Message of
John's Epistles

W. M. Henry

ISBN: 978-1-78364-471-1

www.obt.org.uk

****

THE OPEN BIBLE TRUST
Fordland Mount, Upper Basildon,
Reading, RG8 8LU, UK.

Living in the truth

The Message of John's Epistles

Contents

Page

Introduction: Dimensions of 'the truth'

Introduction: Dimensions of 'the truth'

This study is a brief discussion of one of the major themes of John's epistles – 'the truth.' In his writings John skillfully uses contrasting imagery to great effect – truth and lies; light and darkness; life and death - to compare the way of Jesus Christ with the way of the world. In his epistles he uses the term 'the truth' in a very particular sense to mean a specific body of revelation. He calls on his readers to believe and act upon 'the truth' and teaches that for those who do so it is the key to an unbreakable relationship with God through the Lord Jesus.

This book will consider the theme of 'the truth' as expounded in John's epistles and work through some of the implications of 'the truth' for both our beliefs and our conduct. In addition, it will explore this intimate relationship between the Lord and the believer who lives in 'the truth.'

Although most of the emphasis will be on the three epistles of John, reference will also be made to the passages in his Gospel that impact on the issues being discussed. In interpreting the Scriptures, it is always important to see the way a particular writer uses certain words and phrases to see the special nuances he gives them. For this reason, different passages will be compared to see how they shed light on each other and give us greater insight into the meaning of the passage we are studying.

The writings of John

The writings of John

There are five books in the New Testament which are attributed to John - the gospel, the three epistles and also the book of Revelation. A number of writers have commented on the similarity of imagery, language and structure between the three epistles - it is obvious that they are written by the same person. Also, work has been done to show the parallels between John's Gospel and the *first* epistle of John. For example, John Stott in his commentary on the epistles brings out many of the similarities and concludes that there is very strong evidence for a common authorship of the gospel and the epistles.

So who was the writer of John's gospel? From John 21:20-24 we learn that he was 'the disciple whom Jesus loved' and 'the one who had leaned back against Jesus at the supper,' and this is generally thought to be John.

Living in the Truth 12

The epistles of John

Living in the Truth   14

The epistles of John

In Galatians 2:9 we read that Paul agreed with Peter, James and John that he would concentrate his work on Gentiles and that they would go to the Jews. This would make it likely that John's epistles would have a primarily Jewish rather than a Gentile audience. This is seen most clearly in 1 John 2:2, where we read:

> He is the atoning sacrifice for our sins, and not only for ours but also for the sins of the whole world.

The 'our' and 'ours' refer to the Jews and 'the world' refers to the Gentiles.

This is also borne out by the references in the epistles to gifts of miraculous knowledge (1 John 2:20) and the possibility of immediate judgment on those who commit a sin 'that leads to death' (1 John 5:16), such as happened in the case of Ananias and Sapphira in Acts 5.

There are also references to the imminent return of the Lord Jesus and the work of 'antichrists' (1 John 2:18, 22, 28). These references point to a time of writing during the Acts period, when the hope of Israel was paramount and the return of the Lord Jesus was expected soon. This period ended at Acts 28:28, when Israel was temporarily set aside and the previously unknown purposes of God concerning the church which is Christ's body, were revealed through the apostle Paul.

John's readers, then, were mainly Jewish believers in small churches dispersed throughout the Roman world. It is likely also that they would include some Gentile believers who had been included in Israel's blessings – see Romans 11. However, although the original readership were not people in our situation, all Scripture is profitable and we can learn a great deal of the Lord's will for us from John's writings.

John's first epistle is five chapters in length and is written to give believers assurance that they have eternal life (1 John 5:13). However, the epistle also contains warnings to avoid the teachings of 'antichrists' who will lead believers away from 'the truth.' In addition, the letter is characterised by its teaching on love – love for God and love for fellow believers, which, as John points out in 1 John 2:4-6, is a major part of living in 'the truth.'

John's second epistle is a mere 13 verses and re-iterates John's theme of 'the truth' and its relationship with practical love. The epistle also warns against 'antichrists' and their deceiving heresies, which are contrary to 'the truth'. 2 John is written to 'the chosen lady and her children' who could be real people. However the last verse of 2 John refers to 'the children of your chosen sister' which is an extremely clumsy expression to describe individual people. So the most commonly held view is that the two 'ladies' and their 'children' are two churches, and John is writing from one of them, to the other.

3 John comprises 14 verses but the material is divided into three sections, each revolving round a named individual - Gaius in verses 1-8 is shown as a good example of someone who is 'walking in the truth.' Diotrephes, in contrast, in

verses 9-11 opposes the apostles' authority and is more interested in self-aggrandisement. The third individual, Demetrius, is probably the bearer of the letter and is commended in verse 12. The issues that are raised in John's third epistle are very practical and are concerned, among other things, with the offering of hospitality to visitors.

The epistles are written to a very different world from our own – for example, the problem of apostolic authority is not one that is a major concern of ours. However, the issues to do with relationships within the church family are extremely relevant and the attitude displayed by Diotrephes is depressingly familiar to many of us.

The truth and responses to it

The truth and responses to it

John begins his third epistle by describing himself as 'The elder'. He does not give his name but the title is obviously an important one since it uses the definite article - he is *the* elder. In the first verse of 2 John we find the same title and there has been a lot of discussion as to what it means.

It obviously has a different significance from the way we use the term 'elder' in our own churches and probably indicates a senior member in the community of churches with authority. In Galatians 2:9, Paul describes John as one reputed to be a pillar of the church at Jerusalem – the centre of the Jewish Christian community. So John carries apostolic authority and seems to regard himself as the protector of the purity of the message, which is 'the truth' as he understands it.

The epistle is addressed to 'my dear friend Gaius' (verse 1), who appears to hold quite a responsible position in the church. John writes to him as though he shared John's beliefs and views.

From verses 5-6 we learn that he received visitors and treated them with love and care, even though they were strangers. However, it is apparent from what John writes later about Diotrephes (3 John 9-11), that Gaius is not the leader of the church. Diotrephes seems to have more power within the church than Gaius and is causing damage by the way he wields that power.

John clearly has a high opinion of Gaius and this high opinion is shared by the brothers who reported back to John about him. In verse 3, John speaks of his pleasure at two aspects of Gaius' life:

- his 'faithfulness to the truth' and
- the fact that he is 'walking in the truth'.

At the start, then, we can see the two aspects of 'the truth' – as a body of teaching and as a way of life. The next section explores both of these aspects and how they affect the lives of believers.

Faithfulness to the truth: Truth as a revelation to be believed

Faithfulness to the truth:
Truth as a revelation to be believed

Faithfulness to the truth suggests matters of faith and belief and this idea also appears in 1 John, where 'the truth' is a body of teaching miraculously revealed. In 1 John 2:20 John states:

> But you have an anointing from the Holy One, and all of you know the truth.

But what is this anointing? John continues:

> … the anointing you received from him remains in you, and you do not need anyone to teach you. But as his anointing teaches you about all things and as that anointing is real, not counterfeit – just as it

has taught you, remain in him. (1 John 2:27)

The anointing would appear to be a Spirit-given knowledge. John's phrase "all things" is rather vague but it would appear to be similar to the knowledge written of by Paul in 1 Corinthians 12:8:

> To one there is given through the Spirit the message of wisdom, to another the message of knowledge by the same Spirit.

So what is the context of 'the truth' here? It is something that Gaius and his fellow-believers already know and it concerns the person of Christ. John gives us details in his first letter.

> I do not write to you because you do not know the truth, but because you do know it and because no lie comes from the truth. Who is the liar? It is the man who denies that Jesus is the Christ. Such a man is the antichrist – he denies the Father and the Son. No one who denies the Son has

the Father; whoever acknowledges the Son has the Father also. (1 John 2:21-23)

Later in 1 John, he returns to the theme:

Dear friends, do not believe every spirit, but test the spirits to see whether they are from God, because many false prophets have gone out into the world. This is how you can recognise the Spirit of God: Every spirit that acknowledges that Jesus Christ has come in the flesh is from God, but every spirit that does not acknowledge Jesus is not from God. This is the spirit of the antichrist, which you have heard is coming and even now is already in the world. (1 John 4:1-3)

Here we have another dimension of the Spirit's gifts - an apparent inbuilt ability in the people to whom John was writing to test the true nature of spiritual activity. Again, Paul speaks in 1 Corinthians 12:10 of the gift of "distinguishing between spirits." Here in 1 John, the emphasis is on teaching that denies that Jesus became man.

This warning is also repeated in John's second epistle:

> Many deceivers, who do not acknowledge Jesus Christ as coming in the flesh, have gone out into the world. Any such person is the deceiver and the antichrist. (2 John 7)

The aspect of truth that John focuses on is the person of Christ – and, historically this has been the battleground for centuries. Who is Jesus? Jesus is the Christ, the Son of God, who became man without shedding His deity and died for our sins on the cross. John is concerned about the heretics who were teaching otherwise and he appeals to the believers to hold fast to the truth that is in their hearts.

The basis of this heresy has recurred throughout the history of the Christian church – that Jesus was either mere man (He was not God) or that He was some kind of phantom disguised to look like man (He did not come in the flesh). Even more crudely, in our time, this latter error has shown itself in assertions that Jesus never even existed as a historical figure. Both of these incorrect views of the Lord are dealt with in John's epistles.

John is always careful to explain the historical robustness of the events he describes. He was there; he saw it with his own eyes. See how he begins his Gospel:

> In the beginning was the Word, and the Word was with God, and the Word was God. He was with God in the beginning … The Word became flesh and made his dwelling among **us**. **We** have seen his glory, the glory of the One and Only, who came from the Father, full of grace and truth. (John 1:1,14)

And his first epistle:

> That which was from the beginning, which **we** have heard, which **we** have seen with **our** eyes, which **we** have looked at and **our** hands have touched –

this we proclaim concerning the Word of life. The life appeared; and **we** have seen it and testify to it, and we proclaim to you the eternal life, which was with the Father and has appeared to **us**. We proclaim to you what **we** have seen and heard ... (1 John 1:1-3)

John leaves us in no doubt that the Lord Jesus came in the flesh. He and his friends had seen, heard and touched Him. And in his Gospel, John sets out the evidence for the fact that Jesus is the Christ, that is, the 'Messiah' – the One who had been promised to Israel. Towards the end of the book John writes:

Jesus did many other miraculous signs in the presence of his disciples, which are not recorded in this book. But these are written that you may believe that Jesus is the Christ, the Son of God, and that by believing you may have life in his name. (John 20:30-31)

This is such an important issue. If we do not grasp the truth that the Lord Jesus Christ is both God and man our faith will be diluted and our picture of salvation and God's purposes will be distorted. This is why Satan has constantly attacked the Church on this point and why John is so vehement in his opposition to the error taught by these 'antichrists'

But when we look at passages such as 1 John 2:20,27 quoted above, the revelation of this truth is described as an 'anointing' received from the Spirit and, as a result, John's readers do not need any teachers to learn this truth. Does that apply to us today?

In the period in which John was writing, the Spirit revealed His truth directly to the hearts of believers and through the authoritative teaching of the apostles. In our dispensation, although all Christian truth is spiritually discerned, the Lord reveals Himself primarily through His Word and there is no doubt that, unlike John and his contemporaries, we are very much in need of teachers who give good, sound teaching and exposition of the Scriptures. The truths about the Lord Jesus, however, still stand. Jesus Christ is the same yesterday, today and forever. (Hebrews 13:8).

The consequence of such an authoritative revelation of truth is that those who contradicted the apostles' teaching were not just expressing differences of opinion, but were motivated by spirits other than the Holy Spirit. In his first epistle John tells the Christians of that time that the test as to whether the spirits are from God is whether they acknowledge that Jesus Christ has come in the flesh (1 John 4:1-6). It is for this reason that John argues so strongly that such people should not be welcomed into believers' homes (2 John 10).

John is adamant that following 'the truth' as revealed by the apostles, is the key to a relationship with God. He sets this out in 1 John 4:15:

If anyone acknowledges that Jesus is the Son of God, God lives in him and he in God.

and warns his readers bluntly in 2 John 8-9 and 1 John 2:24:

> Watch out that you do not lose what you have worked for, but that you may be rewarded fully. Anyone who runs ahead and does not continue in the teaching of Christ does not have God; whoever continues in the teaching has both the Father and the Son. (2 John 8-9)

> See that what you have heard from the beginning remains in you. If it does, you also will remain in the Son and in the Father. (1 John 2:24)

In the twenty-first century understanding the truths concerning the Lord Jesus Christ is no less important. His deity is dismissed and ridiculed not only by those outside of the Christian community but, sadly, by many within it. The liberal wing of Christendom has long tried to 'demythologise' the Scriptures and turn the Lord into nothing more than an inspiring and revolutionary teacher who, like many others of His kind, was murdered by the establishment.

More recently however, the seeping of postmodern ideas into the Church has introduced a fluidity of faith, where anything can be deconstructed and re-interpreted if we find it helpful to do so. The historic bedrock truths of the virgin birth, death and physical resurrection of the Lord Jesus can be re-interpreted in a 'spiritual' sense with no reference to the facts.

The reality, as John reminds us, is that our salvation is based on our faith in the work of the Lord Jesus in space and time, some 2,000 years ago in Israel. And our commitment to that truth leads us into a close personal relationship with God Himself and His Son.

The relationship between the Christian, the Father and the Son is an extremely intimate one and the idea of believers 'remaining' in the

Father and the Son is a favourite of John's. This will be explored further when we consider 'walking in the truth' in part 2 of this booklet.

But in his epistles John gives us two contrasting examples of groups of people who believed very different things.

Positive and negative examples: the two groups who went out.

In John's epistles we read of two groups of people who 'went out' from the Christians John represents. The first group were true believers, sent out to build up the local churches. The second group, on the other hand, were turning their backs on the apostles' teaching and, worse than that, were intent on causing problems in the local churches by spreading heresies. The two groups and their conduct stand in stark contrast to each other.

(i) The true believers

We read of the first group in John's third epistle. They had gone from John and his colleagues to visit the churches – or at least the church where Gaius was located, and they reported back the wonderful welcome they received from him. John thanks Gaius for the hospitality shown to these strangers.

> Dear friend, you are faithful in what you are doing for the brothers, even though they are strangers to you. They have told the church about your love … It was for the sake of the Name that they went out, receiving no help from the pagans. We ought therefore to show hospitality to such men so that we may work together for the truth. (3 John 5-8)

Their purpose in visiting the church was to encourage, build up and offer support to these groups of young believers. Therefore they were to be offered hospitality, because they had no other means of support.

The infant churches needed to be built up in their faith and a regular interaction between them seems to have been a means of achieving this, with representatives from one church visiting another to offer encouragement, instruction and even material support where possible. For this to function effectively, the welcoming of visitors in the name of Christ had to be a regular practice. In several of the epistles, we can see Paul and others commending the practice of hospitality as a Christian virtue – e.g. Romans 12:13; 1 Peter 4:9.

(ii) The antichrists

We meet this second group in 1 John 2:18-19:

> Dear children, this is the last hour; and as you have heard that the antichrist is coming, even now many antichrists have come. This is how we know it is the last hour. They went out from us, but they did not really belong to us. For if they had belonged to us, they would have remained

with us; but their going showed that none of them belonged to us.

Three verses later John spells out what the specific doctrinal problem was:

> Who is the liar? It is the man who denies that Jesus is the Christ. Such a man is the antichrist – he denies the Father and the Son. (1 John 2:22)

Here the emphasis is not on the denial that Christ came in the flesh but the denial that Jesus was the Messiah.

As we noted earlier, John speaks in chapter 4 of the *'spirit* of antichrist' and again the critical issue concerns the nature of the Lord Jesus Christ.

> Dear friends, do not believe every spirit, but test the spirits to see whether they are from God…This is how you can recognise the Spirit of God: Every spirit that acknowledges that Jesus Christ is come in

the flesh is from God, but every spirit that does not acknowledge Jesus is not from God. This is the spirit of the antichrist, which you have heard is coming and even now is already in the world. (1 John 4:1-3)

For the churches in John's day, it was imperative that they adhered to sound teaching. Lacking the full New Testament scriptures they were vulnerable to all sorts of ideas. This is why the Lord implanted His truth in their hearts and gave them an anointing to know authentic truth. It is also why John is adamant that they should be on guard against the heretics and not give their teaching the time of day. So how should the churches behave when these 'antichrists' come calling? John tells us in his second epistle:

Many deceivers, who do not acknowledge Jesus Christ as coming in the flesh, have gone out into the world. Any such person is the deceiver and the antichrist … If anyone comes to you and does not bring this teaching, do not take him into your house or welcome him. (2 John 7, 10)

Sound advice – these people need to be shunned and not welcomed into the fellowship of believers.

The advice John gives the believers on how to resist the lie is to trust the truth given to them by the 'anointing of the Holy One" (1 John 2:20). His advice on how to resist the heresy spread by the spirit of antichrist is to 'test the spirits' on the key question of whether Jesus Christ has come in the flesh. This particular issue possibly reflects the growth of Gnostic teaching or the form of religion that glorified the spiritual at the expense of the physical.

Although in our time the issue is not whether Christ came in the flesh (His humanity) but His deity, we also need to test the accuracy of what is being taught by comparing it with the Scriptures. If they do not tally with the Word of God, they are to be rejected, as they are just as much 'anti Christ' as the teaching of the heretics John encountered. Christian believers need to know what they believe and why. They need to have a thorough grasp of God's revelation of

Himself in Christ and in the Scriptures. We are living in a world where there is a cacophony of different ideas competing for our attention and if we do not understand the truths of our faith we are open to a wide range of views that can corrupt our faith and our lives. If we do not know what we believe, we will believe anything.

Walking in the truth: Truth as a life to be lived

Walking in the truth: Truth as a life to be lived

To John, one joy was supreme:

> I have no greater joy than to hear that my children are walking in the truth. (3 John 4)

But what does John mean by 'walking in the truth?' He is building here on the foundation that has been laid down in his earlier epistles. In 2 John 4-6, John explains what 'walking in the truth' means.

> It has given me great joy to find some of your children walking in the truth, just as the Father commanded us. And now, dear lady, I am not writing you a new command but one we have had from the beginning. I ask that we love one another. And this is love: that we walk in

obedience to his commands. As you have heard from the beginning, his command is that you walk in love.

So in practical terms it means living a life characterized by love, in obedience to the Father's command. As he often does in his writing, John constructs a tight network of truths relating to his subject. In this passage we can see the inter-relationship between 'the truth', 'love' and 'obedience.' So in verse 5 we read of this 'new command' which was really there from the beginning, that we should love one another.

John has already reported something similar in his Gospel. In John 13:34 the Lord Jesus says:

A new command I give you: love one another. As I have loved you, so you must love one another.

The Lord Jesus said this to the eleven disciples, who had spent three years in His company, experiencing His self-sacrificial love on a daily basis – a love which ultimately caused Him to lay down His life for His friends. But in 2 John 6 he turns the argument on its head by saying that love is obeying His commands. So we have what appears to be a circular argument: we show love by obedience and the command that we are obeying is the command to love.

The link between love, obedience and the truth is also brought out in John's first epistle:

> We know that we have come to know him if we obey his commands. The man who says, 'I know him' but does not do what he commands is a liar, and the truth is not in him. But if anyone obeys his word, God's love is truly made complete in him. This is how we know we are in him: Whoever claims to live in him must walk as Jesus did. (1 John 2:3-6.)

This passage gives us more insight into John's meaning. As in his second epistle, for John the genuineness of our love *for the Lord* reveals itself in obedience to His command, and the primary command is to love *one another*. God's love is made complete by working itself out through the believer who obeys His command to love his brother. Conversely, if we do not show this obedience and fail to love 'the truth is not in us.'

As the Lord Himself said:

> As the Father has loved me, so have I loved you. Now remain in my love. If you obey my commands, you will remain in my love, just as I have obeyed my Father's commands and remain in his love … My command is this: Love each other as I have loved you. (John 15:9-12)

In the Lord's words we see that, as in 1 John 2:6 quoted above, the believers' love for other Christians is a mirror image of the Lord Jesus' love for them. They are to love one another in the way that He loved them – by laying down their lives for one another, metaphorically or even, if necessary, literally.

John skilfully presents the truth like a many-faceted jewel that he turns round in front of our eyes, so that the light catches it from every angle. He sets before us two walks – two contrasting ways of life. One walk is characterised by obedience, truth, light and love, and the other by disobedience, lies, darkness and hatred.

> If we claim to have fellowship with him yet walk in the darkness, we lie and do not live by the truth. But if we walk in the light, as he is in the light, we have fellowship with one another and the blood of Jesus, his Son, purifies us from all sin. (1 John 1:6-7).

Real knowledge of and love of God demonstrate themselves in walking in obedience to His commands (2 John 5),

> This is love for God: to obey his commands. (1 John 5:3)

and loving our brothers and sisters is what He commands.

> Anyone who claims to be in the light but hates his brother is still in the darkness. Whoever loves his brother lives in the light, and there is nothing in him to make him stumble. But whoever hates his brother is in the darkness and walks around in the darkness; he does not know where he is going, because the darkness has blinded him. (1 John 2:9-11)

But it is not simply a question of walking in light or darkness. There is also the issue of *relationship with God.* In the previous section we saw that believing 'the truth' was key to remaining in the Father and the Son. In addition, John teaches that obedience to the truth, by loving one another, is also the way to establish and maintain this relationship of mutual indwelling between the Father, the Son and the Christian.

God is love. Whoever lives in love lives in God, and God in him. In this way, love is made complete among us so that we will have confidence on the day of judgment, because in this world we are like him. There is no fear in love. But perfect love drives out fear, because fear has to do with punishment. The one who fears is not made perfect in love. (1 John 4:16-18)

So if we live in love we need not fear judgment. If God's love is 'made perfect' or 'made complete' in us we can know that our final destiny is secure. There is no doubt that we are secure in Christ. The issue is that we can have **assurance** and **confidence** that this is the case. This is one of John's main purposes in writing his first epistle. As he says in 1 John 5:13:

> I write these things to you who believe in the name of the Son of God **so that you may know** that you have eternal life.

We have the assurance of the fact that we will not come into condemnation because we are *in*

Him. John's teaching here echoes Paul's triumphant shout of Romans 8:1

> There is now no condemnation for those who are in Christ Jesus.

And, as Paul goes on to explain in Romans 8, the basis on which we recognise our glorious position is by the process of God's Spirit bearing witness with our spirit that we are His children. (Romans 8:16). Similarly in John's writings, the work of the indwelling Spirit is critical in enabling us to experience the reality of revealed truth.

> Those who obey his commands live in him, and he in them. And this is how we know that he lives in us: We know it by the Spirit he gave us. (1 John 3:24)

Our claims to love God, then, only have validity if we love our brothers and sisters. This is how God's love is made 'complete' – when it is transmitted to those we have contact with on a daily basis.

Living in the Truth   54

This is how God showed his love among us: He sent his one and only Son into the world that we might live through him. This is love: not that we loved God, but that he loved us and sent his Son as an atoning sacrifice for our sins. Dear friends, since God so loved us, we also ought to love one another. No one has ever seen God; but if we love one another, God lives in us and his love is made complete in us. (1 John 4:9-12)

God's love for us and our love for our brothers is the same love. First, God showed it to us when He sent the Lord Jesus into the world to give Himself up for fallen humanity. The Lord's love for His Father was expressed in His obedience to Him and in His demonstration of the Father's love not only to the disciples but to all He came in contact with. As a result of the unity between them, He was in the Father and the Father was in Him. Anyone who had seen the Lord Jesus had seen the Father. (John 14:9).

But beyond that, the Lord Jesus offered the disciples (and us) the opportunity to participate in this love relationship. If we, in our turn, love one another with the selfless love of Christ, we are showing the genuineness of our profession of love for Him. Also we are taking the same love of the Father to its completion by impacting directly on the lives of others. If we do this we will remain 'in Him' and He in us just as He remains in the Father and the Father in Him.

In his Gospel, John develops the idea of mutual love being the key to mutual indwelling. In the beautiful section in chapters 14-17, where the Lord gives His final teaching to the disciples before He leaves them to go to the cross, He explains this wonderful truth in detail.

> On that day (resurrection) you will realise that I am in my Father, and you are in me, and I am in you. Whoever has my commands and obeys them, he is the one who loves me. He who loves me will be loved by my Father, and I too will love him and show myself to him. If anyone

loves me, he will obey my teaching. My Father will love him, and we will come to him and make our home with him. (John 14:20-21, 23)

As the Father has loved me, so have I loved you. Now remain in my love. If you obey my commands, you will remain in my love, just as I have obeyed my Father's commands and remain in his love…This is my command. Love each other. (John 15:9, 17)

The extent that we obey the Lord's commands – primarily the command to love – will impact on the extent of the ongoing daily relationship that we will have with Him. If we care little about these things and prefer to pursue our own pleasures and personal interests, we will experience little of the presence of Christ and may lose our reward on the day when we meet Him. In his second epistle John encourages his readers to 'walk in love' (2 John 6) and goes on to warn them of the danger of forfeiting their reward:

Watch out that you do not lose what you have worked for, but that you may be rewarded fully. (2 John 8)

But those who walk with Him in love can participate in a life lived in fellowship with Him. What a privilege we have that God has chosen to bless us in this way! Nothing can take us out of the Lord's hand. We are in Him and He is in us. We need have no fear of condemnation. We are God's children through Christ and we have the power of His Spirit within us confirming His truth to us and assuring us of the reality of our hope. We have a living relationship with Him and the assurance His Spirit brings us of the reality of this truth. Yet, although this is profound in its implications, John tells us that our response to it is rooted in the humdrum reality of our daily lives.

This is how we know what love is: Jesus Christ laid down his life for us. And we ought to lay down our lives for our brothers. If anyone has material possessions and sees his brother in need but has no pity on him, how can the love of God be in him? (1 John 3:16-17).

It is here in the daily grind that the reality or otherwise of our profession of faith in Christ is shown. If we do not demonstrate this love of Christ on a daily basis, then the genuineness of our response to 'the truth' is to be questioned. The primary fruit of the Spirit is love (Galatians 5:22). If there is no sign that that fruit is growing in our lives, there is something seriously wrong with our claims to belong to the Lord.

As we saw in the context of belief, John's third epistle gives us two contrasting examples. Here we have two men who have very different approaches to the working out of the love of God in practice.

Positive and negative examples: Gaius and Diotrephes

Gaius, to whom 3 John is addressed, is commended for 'walking in the truth,' particularly evidenced by the welcome he has given to the brothers who came from John to the church. Diotrephes, on the other hand, is condemned for his love of putting himself first and for refusing to welcome the brothers. As a result, damage was being caused to the church.

(i) Gaius

When we come to 3 John we find a case study of practical love in the actions of Gaius. He showed his love in the way he welcomed the believers who came to his church.

> Dear friend, you are faithful in what you are doing for the brothers, even though they are strangers to you. They have told the church about your love. You will do well to send them on their way in a manner worthy of God. (3 John 5-6)

Gaius had shown real hospitality to the believers sent by John and he is commended for it. The Scriptures places a lot of importance on Christian hospitality. For example, Romans 12:13 tells us to 'practise hospitality'. Widows in particular are encouraged to do this (1 Timothy 5:10) as are church overseers (1 Timothy 3:2). By welcoming people, Hebrews 13:2 says believers sometimes may have entertained 'angels' without realising it and the Lord Jesus says in Matthew 10 that he who receives one of His followers receives Him.

So it is really important. When I was a child I was brought up with the understanding that it was the natural thing to do and we were constantly having visiting preachers and other strangers to stay and I never thought anything of it. And we still try to do it as much as possible. We do not need to own a palace or provide cordon bleu cookery, and I do not think any of the people we entertained were literally angels, but it is an important aspect of Christian service. Of course, not everyone is in a position to do it, but it is highlighted in the New Testament as a mark of a Christian and it is a way of showing the love of Christ to others. So Gaius 'walked in' the truth by showing God's love to his fellow-believers in hospitality.

This is the background against which John writes to Gaius and he is commended for welcoming the brothers presumably sent from John. Even though they were strangers, he obviously looked after them and 'sent them on their way in a manner worthy of God' (verse 6). They had returned to John's church and reported the hospitality they had received from Gaius. 'They have told the church' in verse 6 is in the aorist tense of the verb, which indicates a specific occasion when they reported.

(ii) Diotrephes

But not all people in the church had followed Gaius' example in welcoming the strangers. Diotrephes, who apparently resented what he possibly saw as external interference, preferred to obstruct the work that they were doing, which caused problems both for the visitors and for the church.

He (Diotrephes) refuses to welcome the brothers. He also stops those who want to do so and puts them out of the church. (3 John 10)

Diotrephes, then, was prepared to allow his personal ambitions to interfere with the work of God. There is no suggestion that he disagreed with these people on any doctrinal issue, such as the person of the Lord Jesus, but they came from John and represented a challenge to his leadership and therefore had to be excluded.

John explains the sad situation:

> I wrote to the church, but Diotrephes, who loves to be first, will have nothing to do with us. So if I come, I will call attention to what he is doing, gossiping maliciously about us. Not satisfied with that, he refuses to welcome the brothers. He also stops those who want to do so and puts them out of the church. (3 John 9-10)

As the early local churches developed, individual leaders emerged and in this case (as, no doubt in many) there was a clash between the group under the leadership of Gaius, who were loyal to John and another faction who followed Diotrephes. Gaius' group accepted the apostolic authority while Diotrephes' group resented what they saw as centralised control from Jerusalem and wanted to break free. As William Barclay points out, this was an example of the tension between the universal ministry of the apostles and the local ministry of the elders, and Diotrephes was an elder who seems to have been determined to champion the independence of the local church.

Diotrephes is obviously also in a high position in the church, probably higher than Gaius. He is in a position to influence the people in the church against the believers who came from John and even to put out of the church those who would welcome them. It is not clear whether he has put Gaius out of the church yet, but the situation is probably not irredeemable because John is still in a position to discuss coming to the church to 'call attention' to what he is doing. (verse 10)

So what was his problem? It does not appear to be a doctrinal issue. In his first two epistles John does not hesitate to tackle doctrinal error, so it is unlikely that he would back off from doing so here if there were errors in Diotrephes' teaching. The nub of the problem is in verse 9 - He loves to be first.

Verse 9 indicates that he had blocked an earlier letter from John and that he would have nothing to do with 'us.' It has been suggested that John is referring here to his second epistle, but if that is the case it is really ironic because 2 John warns believers against offering hospitality to false teachers. Unfortunately Diotrephes was refusing to welcome true believers.

So we are dealing with a difficult situation here. The new churches were developing rapidly - some wanted greater freedom and there appears to be a power struggle between the two groups of believers.

Who was right and who was wrong? It is more difficult to decide when there are no doctrinal differences that we can focus on. But it does appear that Diotrephes was in the wrong. We have already noted what was driving him - he loved to be first, which is not a good motive for true Christian service. Paul advises the Philippian Christians to 'do nothing out of selfish ambition or vain conceit' (Philippians 2:3). And if we look at the way Diotrephes behaved, we can see there is something wrong. Look at verses 9-10:

- he will have nothing to do with John and his colleagues
- not only so but he gossips maliciously about them
- refuses to welcome the brothers
- puts those who do welcome them out of the church.

And all because he wanted to be first. And, as John Stott observes, personal vanity still lies at the root of most dissensions in local churches today.

These are not the actions of a true follower of the Lord Jesus. So, in verse 11 John urges Gaius not to behave like that. Instead …

> Dear friend, do not imitate what is evil but what is good. Anyone who does what is good is from God. Anyone who does what is evil has not seen God.

With John there are no grey areas - if you do what is good, it shows you are from God; if your lifestyle is characterized by evil behaviour you have not seen God. As the Lord Jesus said 'by their fruit you will recognise them' (Matthew 7:16). Here in his third epistle, John is again recalling themes he has developed more fully earlier.

> No one who lives in him keeps on sinning. No one who continues to sin has either seen him or known him. (1 John 3:6)

Here in 3 John he says that anyone who continually does what is evil has not seen God.

The closing words of 3 John 11 are virtually identical to what he says in his first epistle. Similar ideas are also set out in 1 John 4:7-8:

> Everyone who loves has been born of God and knows God. Whoever does not love does not know God, because God is love.

It is important to realize that John is not suggesting that we will never do anything wrong. In his first epistle, he pointed out that anyone who says he is without sin is deceiving himself (1 John 1:8). He is not talking about occasional lapses; he is talking about a way of life. The truth is set starkly before us: anyone who continues to sin willfully, deliberately and consistently is demonstrating that he does not really know the Lord at all.

So, John continues:

> No one who is born of God will continue to sin, because God's seed remains in him; he cannot go on sinning, because he

has been born of God. This is how we know who the children of God are and who the children of the devil are: Anyone who does not do what is right is not a child of God; nor is anyone who does not love his brother. (1 John 3:9-10)

There is no escape from it. The behaviour of Diotrephes shows who he really belongs to - the devil - in spite of all his profession and his probable doctrinal soundness. By his behaviour he showed that he was not walking in the truth.

So in 3 John we have 2 case studies: On the one hand we have Gaius, who walks in the truth and demonstrates his obedience to the Lord's command by loving his fellow believers, welcoming them and offering them hospitality; on the other hand we have Diotrephes, who, in spite of his professed belief, displays by his slander and cold-shouldering of the believers who come to him, the fact that he has not seen God.

Selfish ambition is the last reason a Christian should have for aspiring to play a role in Christian leadership. That may be the world's motivation for positions of power but it is a contradiction to the very essence of the Christian message. When He was on the earth, the Lord Jesus repeatedly emphasized this to the disciples. When they argued among themselves on the road as to which of them would be greatest in the kingdom, the Lord's response was to bring a child into their circle and say:

> Whoever welcomes this little child in my name welcomes me; and whoever welcomes me welcomes the one who sent me. For he who is least among you all – he is the greatest. (Luke 9:48)

On another occasion the same argument broke out and the Lord repeated His message:

> The kings of the Gentiles lord it over them… But you are not to be like that. Instead, the greatest among you should be

like the youngest, and the one who rules like the one who serves. (Luke 22:25-26)

The Lord demonstrated this servant attitude Himself in the washing of His disciples' feet in John 13. This, of course was an essential part of showing hospitality to visitors in Christ's day. And what an example it is for us. We are following the Son of Man, who came to serve and to give His life a ransom for many. To do Christian work for prestige or personal ambition indicates that we haven't understood the nature of it at all.

The motivation must be to serve - and we can be glad and eager to have the opportunity to use our gifts and talents in the Lord's service - but if it's an ego trip or to acquire praise or admiration or status, then it's a waste, because it's not service at all. Such an attitude shows that we, like Diotrephes, are not walking in the truth.

In conclusion ...

In conclusion ...

As far as the believer is concerned, then, there are two aspects to our response to 'the truth,' – truth as believed and truth as practised on a daily basis. Both are necessary for fellowship with the Lord. Without belief in His Son, the Lord Jesus, there can be no relationship with the Father because we are not 'faithful to the truth'; if we fail to love one another in obedience to Jesus' command, it is a sign that we do not truly love Him and the intimacy is lost. But if we embrace the truth and put it into practice on a daily basis, the Lord has promised that, by His Spirit, He will bring us into the personal love relationship that exists within the Godhead. Such claims are astonishing yet many down through the centuries have been able to testify to the reality of that experience.

John, in his epistles, gives us a series of contrasting examples to illustrate the points he is making. In relation to doctrine, he describes the work of the true believers, who travelled from church to church re-enforcing the truth and building up the faith of Christians in the churches they visited. He also warns against the other group who "went out", whom he describes as antichrists. Far from building up the churches, they tried to undermine the message of the truth with an incorrect doctrine about the nature of the Lord Jesus Christ.

In relation to the practical response to truth, we have the positive example of Gaius, who practised hospitality and welcomed the itinerant teachers into the church, and the negative example of Diotrephes, who, fired by personal ambition, refused to accept them and encouraged others to do the same.

In these examples we can see the different responses to the truth. The Lord asks us to believe it and also to work it out in our lives on a daily basis. Faith and obedience are two sides of the same coin. They are the appropriate responses to the truth as it is in Jesus. In 1 John 3:23 we can see the two aspects coming together, when John writes of God's command:

This is his command: to believe in the name of his Son, Jesus Christ, and to love one another as he commanded us.

If we concentrate on one, at the expense of the other, we are not really grasping the nature of the truth – it has to be both believed and lived. But if we engage with both responses to the truth our lives will be transformed by His presence and we can walk in a living fellowship with Him and with the Father.

About the author

W. M. Henry was born in Glasgow in 1949. He qualified as a Chartered Accountant and worked in the accountancy profession for a number of years before moving into academia. He is now retired and lives in Giffnock with his wife and two daughters. He is an international speaker and has spoken in Canada, Australia and the Netherlands. He has recently had published a major book, *The Trinity in John*: see later for details.

Other publications by W M Henry include:

The Signs in John's Gospel
Covenants: Old and New
No Condemnation – Romans 5:12-8:39
Living in the Truth
That you may know – 1 John
The Speeches in Acts ..... By Faith Abraham
The Making of a Man of God ..... Imitating Christ

W M Henry has also written a number of books with Michael Penny including:

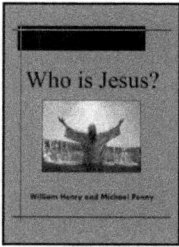

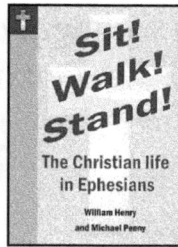

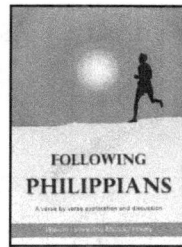

Who is Jesus?
A study based on Matthew 16:13-16

The Will of God: Past and Present.
In the Bible and in the 21st Century

Sit! Walk! Stand!
The Christian life in Ephesians

Following Philippians
A verse by verse exploration and discussion

Further details of these can be seen on
www.obt.org.uk
And they can be ordered from that website.

They are also available
as eBooks from Amazon and Apple and
as KDP paperbacks from Amazon

Living in the Truth

W M Henry is a frequent contributor to *Search* magazine

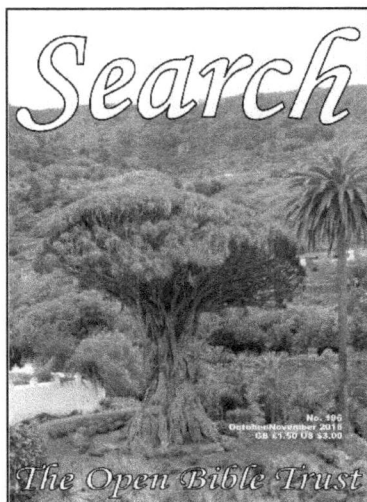

Also by W M Henry

The Trinity in John
A study in relationships

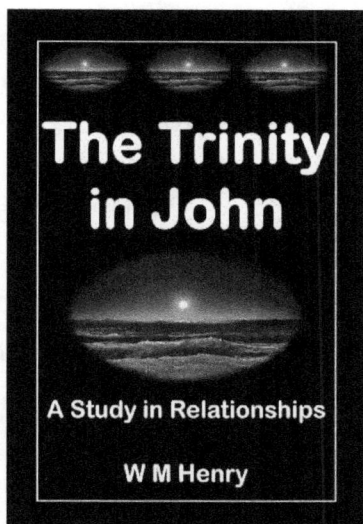

This book is a study of the relationships between the members of the Trinity and between the Trinity and Christian believers, focusing mainly on the Gospel of John.

It opens with a discussion of the titles given to the Lord Jesus in John's Gospel and what they tell us about His relationship with His Father.

Section two explores the relationship between the Father and the Son and their joint work of redemption.

The book then widens the focus to examine the relationship between the Father, the Son and the believer before discussing the Holy Spirit and His relationship with other members of the Trinity, and with the believer.

Each chapter closes with brief meditative "Reflections" on the implications of the issues raised in the chapter. These are followed by suggestions for further study, which can be the basis for private devotions or group discussions.

****

All the publications mentioned in this book can be ordered from **www.obt.org.uk** or from

The Open Bible Trust, Fordland Mount, Upper Basildon, Reading, RG8 8LU, UK.

They are also available as eBooks from Amazon and Apple and as KDP paperbacks from Amazon

****

About this book

Living in the Truth
The Message of John's Epistles

This study is a discussion of one of the major themes of John's epistles – 'the truth.' In his writings John skillfully uses contrasting imagery to great effect:

- truth and lies;
- light and darkness;
- life and death.

He does this to compare the way of Jesus Christ with the way of the world.

In his epistles he uses the term 'the truth' in a very particular sense, to mean a specific body of revelation. He calls on his readers to believe and act upon 'the truth', for to do so is the key to an unbreakable relationship with God through the Lord Jesus.

Publications of The Open Bible Trust must be in accordance with its evangelical, fundamental and dispensational basis. However, beyond this minimum, writers are free to express whatever beliefs they may have as their own understanding, provided that the aim in so doing is to further the object of The Open Bible Trust. A copy of the doctrinal basis is available on **www.obt.org.uk** or from:

THE OPEN BIBLE TRUST
Fordland Mount, Upper Basildon,
Reading, RG8 8LU, UK.

www.ingramcontent.com/pod-product-compliance
Lightning Source LLC
Chambersburg PA
CBHW070554030426
42337CB00016B/2497